Handbook
for
your
Blind Date

"A blind date is a meeting with a person you have not met before, arranged in the hope of starting a romantic relationship"—Little Oxford Dictionary.

Preface

So you are thinking about going on a blind date with that person you have been communicating with over the phone or internet. The person seems to be the type you would start a romantic relationship with. And now you are contemplating on how you will go about meeting him or her. A lot of questions are popping up in your mind. What are you to do? What are you to wear? What if this? What if that?

Relax. This little book will guide you.

Self assessment

Self assessment is important before taking on anything that will affect the way your life functions. So first of all, before the blind date, you must take some time to asses yourself using four important questions. These are very important questions which must be given proper thought.

- <u>Am I at a time in my life for a blind date?</u>

Remember, a blind date is a meeting arranged in the hope of starting a romantic relationship. So you must take into consideration your:

(a) **Emotion:** Believe it; a romantic relationship is built upon emotion. If you have not gotten over your ex (or still holding on to baggage from your last relationship), you are not emotionally ready to start a romantic relationship.

(b) Age: Nothing is wrong with having a 'crush' on a guy or girl at school. But you may not want to be starting a romantic relationship under age 16. This is because most teenaged romantic relationships never lasted into adulthood, typically discarded into history by one partner as 'school romance.'

The question of whether or not you are 'too old' is also a significant one. But, respectfully, no one is too old for love and companionship. So if you are 85 years old and reading this book, keeping reading on grandma.

- <u>Am I really ready to share my personal life with another person?</u>

How ready your personal life is will determine how the other person will fit into it. Being single means living a life for one (self). Getting into a romantic relationship means getting into a life for two (you and your partner). Before you get into a romantic relationship, you should first throw off habits which are 'only for me' and replace them with things that are mutual in manner. You must throw off simple but relationship-wrecking habits such as leaving laundry on the floor, leaving the toilet seat up, inviting over friends too often, cleaning your teeth at the kitchen sink, leaving the toothpaste container open, etc. Some personal habits may not be pleasant to the other person in a romantic relationship. Those habits are OK to the 'me' but will be a nuisance to the 'us.'

The main thing from your personal life that you must prepare to share in a romantic relationship is **your time**. Being single, you probably spend most of your time alone, at work, with relatives, or with friends. Getting into a romantic relationship means you will have to create time for it in order for it to work. The other person will not want to be in your life as a title—your boyfriend or girlfriend. Such person will need your time.

Nobody can give another person all his or her time. Therefore you will fit the other person (your partner) into your time in a balanced way. You will do this by reducing times with friends, relatives, etc to time with your partner. If the both of you have to work long hours, there must be those 'times for us.'

- Am I ready to be true and faithful to only one person?

You are not ready for a romantic relationship until you decide to have only one sex partner. If you are sleeping around while starting a romantic relationship, you are not genuinely looking for a romantic partner—you are just looking for a 'main sex partner.' A romantic relationship is a relationship which clearly says "only the two of us, excluding any other." If you create the condition of a romantic relationship with a person, typically, such person will not expect you to be sleeping with someone else.

- ## What is the type of person that should make me happy?

The other person is of interest to you. This is very reason why you will go on the blind date. However, notwithstanding what you already understood about the person you will meet, you must have a clear understanding of what type of person will make you happy.

Take the time to think about who would make your ideal partner, even writing down the qualities you want in such a person. You must note all the significant things which would make you happy in a romantic relationship. For example, you enjoy oral sex and partying at the club on weekends. If you start a romantic relationship with someone who does not like these things, there will be a problem.

You will need to find your type of partner in a person who enjoys activities that are dare to you. It is a mistake to think that a person's appearance (hair colour, height, etc) and job will make you happy. A person's job and appearance are worth consideration, but these things will not bring lasting happiness. The reason why most romantic relationships/marriages broke up was because they were built mainly round physical appearances and job positions. What happiness will you have in a romantic relationship with a rich and handsome guy who does not want you to leave the house or accompany him to any public event?

While there is arguably nothing called the 'perfect partner,' you must have a clear understanding of the type of person who should make you happy. When you have made a note of such type of person, ask yourself the following question: **Am I suitable for such type of person?** You cannot search for an over-qualified partner for an under-qualified self. This would be like searching for a medical job, when you are only qualified to work as a janitor. For example, you cannot want a "sweet, loving and caring woman" when you are a guy who smokes and swears every day.

To suit your ideal mate, you must alter to fit. You must change in your life the things which would change the other person's mind from you. If you are not willing to alter to fit, then the best alternative is to try finding someone who is just like you---meaning that if you drink, smoke and regularly use profanities, find someone who is like that.

When wanting a romantic partner to make you happy, remember that happiness in any relationship comes from mutual contribution.

Convenient Time

Make your blind date special, which it should be, by arranging for it to happen at a mutually convenient time. You should not set your blind date at a time when you will not have enough time for it. What does the term 'enough time' means here? You should not arrange your blind date for a time when your mind would be busy thinking about getting something else done. A blind date needs time for both parties to greet, relax, and understand each other. You should not be thinking "I have only 20 minutes for this before getting to the gym."

If a blind date will be restricted by time, choose another time.

Internet Blind Date

The internet has become such a convenient place for many things---buying, selling, donating, paying bills, making friendship, etc—that it seems so appropriate for a blind date. The ability for two persons to see, hear, and speak to each other live makes the contact feels complete. But it is not complete and reassuring. You cannot truly date someone by looking at them through a computer or phone screen. A blind date requires both individuals to meet in person, smell each other, and touch each other with only steps apart.

An internet blind date is finite. Any progressive individual who thinks a blind date can be conducted via the internet will be blind to who the other individual truly is.

Contents

Safety Tips

Without having to decrease the excitement in you, it is judicious that you apply precaution while you go on a blind date. The world is operated on a balance of good and evil. While you desire good, evil can affect you at any point in your life—even on a blind date. So here are some useful precautions that are applicable.

- **Meet at a safe place**

A 'safe place' is a place that is public, a place where you can be seen or heard in case of danger. It is not just important to meet in a safe place, but staying in the safe place is equally significant. Many times individuals met in a safe place and one allowed the other to coax him or her into another place where something bad happened. If you meet your date in a public park, for example, you should not be persuaded to go to a place where no one else can hear you if something went wrong.

While you want to enjoy the special occasion, you want to at the same time ensure that you do not get hurt by a criminal hiding behind a 'nice guy' or 'friendly woman' façade.

- **Tell someone where you are going**

If you will meet the other person out of town, in an unfamiliar place, you should tell at least one person where you are heading to and even who you will meet. If you do not want to tell anyone where you are going, you may write a note in which you state exactly where you are going, the date, and who you will meet. Leave the note conspicuously in your bedroom or drawer.

- **Do not meet at your house**

It is not advisable to direct the other person to your home. Not knowing someone fully and inviting them to your house is risky. You do not want to be finding out about the other person while he or she is sitting in your living room.

The same advice applies in reverse—do not meet the other person at his or her home. It is not that you do not trust your date. The point is that there have been stories of rape, kidnapping, etc from individuals dating persons they thought they knew.

- **Do not wear expensive jewelry**

An expensive jewelry triggers a negative thought—the thought to steal it. An expensive jewelry not only encourages feigned love, it makes you a target for robbery.

Proper Hygiene

There is an adage which goes "first impression lasts." If you turned up to your blind date looking like someone who does not take good care of him or herself, you may ruin the possibility for a romantic relationship. You would not want the other person to think: "If he/she does not care about self, why would he/she care about me?" Because a blind date is a special meeting, each party must give the best representation of self. This means that you will pay much attention to how you will smell and look.

Wash and scrub yourself

If you never used to scrub while bathing, this is the time to do so. You will need to scrub behind the ears, between the buttocks, around the feet, across the back, etc. Spend some time on your finger nails by cleaning them thoroughly. No matter how clean your clothes are dirty-looking fingernails are a turn off.

Brush Your Teeth

_A clean mouth will not repel a kiss. Before you go on your blind date, brush your teeth and do not eat anything before you meet the other person. It would not look good if you smile and the other person sees a piece chewed pork stuck between your front teeth.

Use body care products

_It would be nice to bathe with a soap that will leave your body smelling fresh. And especially if you have dry skin, apply lotion to your body. The use of a perfume would be an excellent addition.

Groom your hair

Groom your hair (if you are not bald headed) to enhance your appearance. Hair grooming includes beard and moustache. If you have hair growing out of the nose, this is the time to cut them out with a small pair of scissors. Your date would not want to look at your nose and see strands of hair waving "Hello."

When you have done all you can to look and smell your best, do not become self-conscious. You will never know what your date will think until he or she expresses an opinion.

----- ------ -----------

What Not To Wear

You will meet the other person for the first time. The person—even though you both have been communicating for a while—does not 'know' you. Therefore you should not wear any of the following identity-masking things:

<u>Sunglasses</u>

You should not approach the other person wearing sunglasses. The first place a person looks when they meet you is in your eyes. If the other person cannot see your eyes, he or she may feel uncomfortable with you.

Hood

If you wear a shirt with a hood, you should drop the hood before approaching (or being approached) by your date. Because hoods are many times used by criminals masking their identities, many individuals associate a hood with criminals, thugs, or gang members.

Wig and fake eyelashes

If you think you need a wig and fake eyelashes to look beautiful for your date, then you do not believe in the power of natural beauty. The truth is, when you wear fake lashes and wig, you are masking your true identity. You are trying to tell your date that the spurious appearance is 'my beauty.' If you truly want a lasting romantic relationship with a guy, you should face him with your real look. Otherwise when you remove that wig and fake lashes—he will be running through the door.

What To Wear

What should I wear? Maybe you ask this question in front a closet full of clothes or maybe in front a small and shabby box with little bric-a-brac. Whichever it is in your case, where you will meet—and your age—will determine the type of clothes you should put on. Also take into consideration the type of person your date is and dress according to what you best think he or she will like.

Dress modestly

It is best to play it safe regarding what you will wear by dressing modestly. You might think that dressing in a mini skirt and a cleavage-exposing blouse with a pair of high heeled boots is sexy—but you might end up coming across to your date as slutty.

If you are a male, you might think that wearing your pants below your waist and putting on a cap in reverse make you look cool—but your date might think "this is not the type of guy I want my friends or parents to see me with."

Playing it safe with what you wear means that you will put on clothes that cannot easily send the wrong impression to your date. Remember, importantly, that the clothes you wear will introduce you to your date even before you say "hi." Your clothes play a part in how you are regarded. When you go on the streets, you can easily identify a policeman, nurse, or a nun by the clothes they wear. You will think that the guy who just passed you with his big jeans below his waist and a hood drawn over his head is a thug, because of how he is clothed. Now, the question is: What do you want your date to think when he or she sees you approaching?

The way a person dresses will make another thinks of him or her as cool, intelligent, sloppy, fashionable, nerdish, religious, or business-like. Now, which of these impressions would you like your date to have of you when he or she first sets eyes on you in person?

If based on your communication with your date you know that he or she is business-like, for example, you should choose attire that you best believe fits such type of person.

Your age

You should choose clothing that is age-appropriate. If your date is religious, for example, this does not mean you should dress looking like a grandmother or grandfather for the blind date. If your date is far younger than you (example, you are 50 and he/she is 29), you do not need to dress to look   like someone in his/her twenties. Not dressing age-appropriate might make you look out of kilter to your date.

NB: When you are not certain about what clothes from your wardrobe will impress your date, the best thing is to dress modest.

Greeting Each Other

No matter how long you both have been communicating over the phone or internet, communication face to face brings a different impression. When you greet someone face to face, that person is getting a lot more signals from you than he or she was getting over the internet or phone. The person is now getting messages from your facial expressions, your oral and physical smell, and touch of your hands— while at the same time fathoming your disposition. So follow these steps as you greet:

<u>Start with a compliment</u>

It is best to commence your conversation with a compliment. But you should avoid references that only lovers use—such as 'baby,' 'honey,' or 'sexy.' Starting off by referring to your date as honey, for example, might give your date the impression that this is something you do with other men or women. Your date might want to 'know' you first before feeling comfortable with you referring to him or her the way lovers do. So you should start with a simple but polite compliment.

On the following page is a simple example between Sally and David, which shows you how you might start your blind date with a compliment:

David: Hello, Sally.

Sally: Hi, David.

David: You look gorgeous tonight.

Sally: (smiling) Thanks

David's compliment of Sally's appearance gives her a pleasant feeling and thus makes their conversation much comfortable henceforth.

What Not To Do During the Date

Your blind date may be formal or informal. A formal blind date would be one that is arranged for—example—a fancy restaurant where you both have to be dressed formally and adhere to the etiquette of eating with a knife and a fork. An informal blind date, on the other hand, would occur where there is no special rule (dress code) regarding what you both wear and behave. An informal blind date may occur almost anywhere—on a beach, inside a KFC restaurant, outside a shopping mall, in a park, etc.

There are things you should not do during the blind date. Remember that you are going to meet the other person for the first time. That person will construct an opinion of you base on pretty much everything you do and say. Whether you will be thought of as loving, too religious, gullible, dull or plain disgusting will depend on your own behaviour. So the following are the 'Don'ts' on your blind date.

Do not tell all that you are looking for in a person

Do not tell your date all that you are looking for in a soul mate. If the person is no-good, he or she might just pretend to be the type of person you are looking for, temporarily, to get what they want. You will not want to give the impression that you are gullible.

Do not be loquacious

You should be a good listener and never try to control the conversation. You will want to let your date feel relaxed in your company. In the blind date, let the conversation be free to you and your date. Nobody likes to be in a conversation where the other person is just yacking away. By giving space for your date to speak, you make the conversation mutual.

If you noticed that your date is reticent or laconic, you will have to become somewhat interrogative, asking questions like: How was your bus ride getting here? This is a lovely place, how do you like it so far?

Do not waste the time to learn more about your date

Overall, the blind date is arranged for you to learn more about the other person and allow him or her to learn more about you, face to face. So you should ask the person things you would want to know about him or her—such as future plans (example: children, career, etc), religion, hobbies, and so on. But you must not throw all the questions at your date at once. Space out your questions during the blind date.

Do not stare

While it is a show of confidence to make eye contact with your date, it is not a pleasant thing to stare at the person. No one likes to see another person staring at him or her.

Do not pick your nose

Picking your nose on a blind date is like a waiter choosing to carry out the garbage between dining customers. Nose-cleaning is something that you should do while preparing yourself at home. While cleaning your teeth or behind your ears, you must also clean your nose. This will ensure that you have no reason to poke a finger up your nostril while conversing with your date. Because many individuals find nose-picking in public disgusting, you should not run the risk of turning off your date.

Do not grin without an apparent reason

You must never grin or laugh without an apparent (or appropriate) reason. Apart from this portraying you as silly, or becoming an offence to your date, it is not a 'mature' thing to do. Because you are meeting the other person face to face for the first time, you must evade giving the impression that you are silly or rude.

Do not pass wind

While it is a natural, God-made thing to belch or let out intestinal wind, your blind date is not an appropriate meeting to do such thing. The other person is meeting you for the first time. Belching out loud after a drink or releasing a malodorous wind will likely cause your date to think: "I never want to meet this person again."

Do not chew with open mouth

Many persons are irked by someone masticating with open mouth. Since you do not know if your date is one of such persons, you should avoid chewing with open mouth.

Also, you should not gulp. And if you will drink soap, do not suck in noisy air while you drink. Your date might be irked by the sound from such an act.

Do not speak about personal problems

The purpose of a blind date is for two persons to build on the possibility of a romantic relationship by learning more about each other face to face. This might sound like the right time to reveal personal problems to your date. Indeed, you are allowing the other person to learn more about you. But, importantly, a blind date is not the meeting to bring up a personal problem—such as, for example, the bills you cannot afford to pay from last month. If you let your life sounds problematic, the other person might not want to be a part of it.

Do not ask an opinion of you

You might be tempted to ask the other person what he or she thinks of you at the end of the blind date. You are hereby encouraged not to do that.

The other person might need time to make a concrete decision about commencing a romantic relationship with you. Yes, the person might have enjoyed your company. But the person might need more time to say whether or not you are 'the one.' So do not ask--just leave things to time, a few days at least.

If the person still answers your calls, or calls you, after the blind date, this means that he or she still holds an interest in you.

If you texted or called, even left a voice message, and the person did not respond, he or she has most likely decided against starting a romantic relationship with you.

NB: Many romantic relationships did not start with the first date. The other person may not make a firm decision about you until after a second date. Do not feel that it is unnecessary to go on a second date. Sometimes it takes another sip of a good wine to fall in love with the flavour.

Things To do During the Date

To give a pleasant representation of yourself, here are some things you should do during the date:

Have only beautiful thoughts

You must have a positive attitude going into your blind date. You should not go on your blind date looking lethargic, upset or worried. No matter how your night or day has been, you will need to have an upbeat sound and appearance for your date.

Smile

When you smile, you give your face a pleasant expression. It is recommended that you smile the very second you make eye to eye contact with your date, because this is the crucial point to how you both will regard each other onward. A smile will send off a 'nice guy' or 'nice woman' impression in the direction of your date. Your smiling countenance makes your date immediately thinks that you are approachable.

It is not a necessity that you smile throughout the entire meeting. You can release the smile, reaching back for it again as is necessary.

Be open apart yourself

You are on the blind date for the other person to learn more about you face to face. So you cannot be a closed book to your date. You must provide information about yourself to your date. The extent to which you will be open to your date will depend on you. You know the things about your own life that you are comfortable with revealing from the things which you know are best left untold.

But you will need to let your date know things like your favourite colour, hobbies, likes and dislikes in a romantic relationship, religion and occupation. It is also important to be honest about whether you are single, divorced or going through a divorce. You must tell your date whether or not you have a child and whether or not you have your own place (home).

There are things you should not voluntarily reveal. That is, you will not reveal these things unless you are directly asked. Such things include—for example—prison time you have served, an abortion, or you used to work as a prostitute.

Have fun together

Your blind date is supposed to be exciting. You are to make it exciting. It might be dull for the both of you to sit down at a table throughout the entire meeting. A blind date is not like a boring meeting with a droning boss. The both of you should spice up the blind date beyond the just 'sit and talk.'

If you meet your date inside a library, for example, do not just sit at the table the whole time. The both of you can browse books together, then stroll outside to a nearby restaurant for two meals together before standing somewhere on a street and just enjoy watching the traffic. By including a variety of activities to your blind date, you get to know different sides to the other person while really having fun.

To Have or Not To Have Sex

Is sex wrong on a blind date? This is the weighty question to the above topic of whether to have or not to have sex on a blind date.

It must first be emphatically understood that there is nothing wrong with sex. It is a gift by nature for pleasure and reproduction. But the question of where, when and who to have sex with must be carefully contemplated. A result from a sexual activity might not be pleasant. Unwanted pregnancy, STDs, and the tarnishing of one's reputation are just some of the commonly nefarious consequences of unwise sex.

It is hard if not impossible to correctly say it is right or wrong to have sex on a blind date. Some blind dates have engaged in sex and are still together after many years. Other blind dates who have engaged in sex regret having done it.

Whether or not you will have sex on the first face to face meeting depends on the type of individual you are or the type of person your date is.

Type of person you are

If you are the type of individual who is not reserving sex for the special partner you hope to find, or you are one of those men or women who is easy-to-get, then the likelihood of you getting butt naked with your date is high.

Type of person your date is

The type of person your date is might be the very reason why you have sex with him or her on the blind date. From the very second you set eyes on your date in person, you might be thinking "gosh, he (or she) is so hot." Your date might be so sexy and likeable that you just think: "What the heck, let's just do it." This would not mean that you are a slut or a womanizer. This would just be one of those times in your life when you let your hair down (temporarily ignore some of the standards by which you behave) and just have fun. Apparently, you have only one life. So why not dive into some adventurous fun now and again?

Whether or not sex would be right or wrong on your blind date is not the concern. If you conclude that the other individual is right for you, then sex is right. If you have that feeling that the individual is wrong for you, sex is wrong.

You Be The Judge

Only you must be the judge of whether or not your date was worth the time and preparation that you have put into that first face to face meeting. It is OK to go to a trusted relative or friend and talk about the blind date and hear their opinion about the other person. Sometimes the opinion of a good friend helps shape the right decision.

However, it was your date. It is your life. Only you must make the final decision whether the other person is right for you. When you listen to your own heart regarding your date, you will make the decision that makes you happy.